iOS 12 for iPad

The Answer to All Your IOS 12 Questions

Table of Contents

Introduction

Congratulations on purchasing this book! This book was designed for you as an iPad user to help you get the most out of your device with Apple's newest operating system and the many new features being introduced with it.

In *iOS 12 for iPad: The Answer to All Your IOS 12 Questions*, you will learn about all of the incredible features being added to your device to enhance your user experience and fall in love with your device even more! This operating system upgrade is a massive milestone for Apple, taking us officially out of the several iOS 11 updates and into a brand-new system. As such, they have included many great features to truly give us a next-level experience with our Apple devices.

In this book, I am going to help you understand how all of these changes will impact your experience with your iPad, as well as how you can navigate and take full advantage of the latest additions. Through this guide, you will be given the opportunity to get reacquainted with your device and maximize your usage. This will ensure that you get the most out of the new iOS 12 operating system!

You will notice that each chapter has been designed to help you get acquainted with the new operating system and what the changes mean for you. We will start by exploring the basic features so that you have an idea of all that your device is capable of already. Then, we will explore the brand-new features that will make all of these basic features next-level! Finally, I will show you how to control and customize all of the new features so that you can have the best iOS 12 experience possible.

Consider this the only go-to guide you will ever need to understand iOS 12 for your iPad! Keep it handy on your device so that you can access it at any time. That way, if you find that you have any questions as you begin using your new system, you can simply click to the appropriate page in this guide and be walked through the experience. And of course, be sure to enjoy!

Chapter 1
Basic Features

iPads are an incredible tool that features exceptional versatility. People purchase them for every purpose, from being able to stay up-to-date with their latest books and news on social media to using them as check-out terminals at their shops. iPads are powerful, handy, and capable little devices that can perform a myriad of tasks.

Each year, a new generation of the iPad is released for Apple fans to purchase and use. The device gets better every year; however, it does have some standard basic features that we see on every generation that comes out. These basic features make the iPad reliable, easy to navigate, and high-powered.

In case you are new to the iPad, we are going to take some time to explore these features now. Understanding what these features are and how they work will ensure that you understand how they are being impacted by the latest iOS 12 operating system update. If you already know about the basic standard features of your device, you may wish to skip over this chapter and move on to the latter chapters.

Retina Display

When Apple introduced the 3rd generation iPad, they also introduced the retina display screen. This retina display means that they have made each individual pixel so small that the naked eye cannot distinguish one from the other. It means that you no longer have a pixelated view of anything on your screen. The viewing quality is so high that it does not even feel like you are looking at a screen in many cases. It is the clearest possible quality you can get on a screen, and it comes standard on every iPad after the 3rd generation release.

Multi-Touch Display

All iPads come with what is known as multi-touch display as a standard feature. This multi-touch display means that you can touch the screen with multiple fingers, and your device has the capacity to recognize each individual touch. You might have noticed how, on some other devices, the device doesn't respond when you use more than one fingertip. Or if that isn't what happens, it may instead begin functioning oddly, acting as though you have touched something that you did not intend to touch on the screen. This is because, without the proper multi-touch display, touch screens cannot process the touch of multiple surfaces; they are usually limited to only one point. While the iPad cannot perform or launch multiple functions at once (for example, if you try to increase the brightness slide and try to launch the Internet at the same time, the device will not know what to do and will likely do nothing), with the multi-touch display, your device can recognize when multiple fingers are touching the screen. In fact, it actually relies on this sensor to perform certain convenience functions, such as zooming or swiping between applications or using other touch prompts that require more than one finger to perform.

Motion Co-Processor

The motion co-processor is the piece of the device that is responsible for making the multi-touch display possible. The motion co-processor comes standard in every single iPad device, meaning that all iPads are capable of using the multi-touch display technology. The motion co-processor is the hardware that makes the multi-touch display software usable, and vice versa. This hardware comes standard-built in every single iPad, as it provides the basis for many of the convenient touch features available on iPad devices.

Dual-Facing Cameras

When Apple launched the iPad 2, they also introduced the dual-facing cameras in the device. This feature then became a standard feature across all iPads that have launched since the iPad 2. This means that every iPad comes standard with one camera in the front (often referred to as a selfie camera), which Apple actually specifically designed to optimize FaceTime video conferencing for the iPad. This camera is intended to make it easy for you to be seen by those in your conference call while effortlessly using the screen to navigate the call or other features on your device at the same time. The second camera comes in the back of the iPad, and it is used for taking portrait and landscape pictures. This camera was upgraded from a 5-megapixel camera to an 8-megapixel camera when the dual-facing cameras were introduced, and it is capable of taking videos in 1080p quality. All of the cameras on the iPad devices are now equipped with the 8-megapixel camera and a 1080p filming quality. This means that both cameras on your device are the highest quality they have ever been on iPad devices, often outperforming the cameras on most other comparable devices. They are also highly effective at helping you perform any task you desire with your camera, making it easy to see the screen from almost any angle.

Dual Microphones

In addition to dual-facing cameras, the iPad also comes equipped with dual microphones. This means that instead of coming equipped with just one microphone, your device actually has two next to each other, located on the bottom where previously, on older devices, only one microphone was located. Having two microphones on the device means that your iPad is capable of hearing you over any background noise that may be surrounding you. It makes it so that the sound of your microphone that is being projected into your video, call, or recording is clear and easy to hear. While it cannot completely cancel out background noise, it does make it significantly easier for you to be heard when you are speaking into your device through the microphones. This means your film and call audio are in higher quality, making the iPad a great device for taking with you on-the-go, as you can perform conference calls or record videos anywhere from a quiet hotel room to a busy coffee hut.

Proximity and Ambient Light Sensors

Because of the camera on the front of the device, the iPad is capable of measuring ambient lighting in any room, allowing it to automatically adjust the brightness of your screen accordingly. The camera is virtually always measuring the ambient light in the room that you are in. This does not mean, though, that the camera is constantly on and watching you. This is simply a light sensor, similar to those in the floodlights that people use in their yards or in office buildings, to help you get the best-quality viewing display. This ambient light sensor allows your iPad to create a clearer display for you to view, which is much easier for your eyes. It works by raising the brightness in brighter areas, where you will need more backlight to see the screen, and lowering the brightness in darker areas, where you need less backlight to see the screen. It also preserves battery power, since you are not using more brightness than you actually need to view the screen with. Furthermore, this makes the device easier on your eyes, as you will not be accidentally viewing a screen that is too bright in a dark room, which can cause damage to your eyes, along with a myriad of other problems such as insomnia and restlessness at night when you are trying to sleep.

Lightning Connector

Through the upgrades, Apple eliminated the 30-pin connector with the lightning connector. The newer lightning connector is significantly smaller and is interchangeable between all of the new Apple products. You will use this single cable for everything when it comes to plugging your iPad in or connecting it to other devices, such as your computer. This cord is smaller, more reliable, and a lot safer, as well. The lightning connector charges your device faster, improves connectivity speed, and does not heat up as much as the 30-pin connector did.

Some people wonder why Apple went for the lightning connector as opposed to the popular micro-USB connector that most other devices (outside of Apple) use. One of the reasons why the lightning cable has been chosen over the micro-USB is that the cable is more reliable. Micro-USB cables break down over time, causing users to have to sit the cord "just right" for it to work. Lightning cables are not at risk of having these problems, meaning they last much longer, and you do not run into as many issues with your charging port. They are also convenient as you do not have to position them a certain way for them to fit into your device. There is no "right-side-up" with a lightning cable. Additionally, due to the maximized power of the charger, they can charge virtually anything from an iPhone to a MacBook. They are clearly a lot more powerful and efficient than the alternative connectors.

External Speaker

The iPad has always come with an external speaker; however, they have improved the speakers significantly over the years. Originally, the iPad came equipped with a single external speaker that was featured on the very bottom of the iPad. This speaker was lower quality and was incapable of producing as much volume as modern iPad speakers do. When they introduced the new lightning cable charging ports, Apple also split the external speaker into two. Now, a single external speaker is located on either side of the lightning connector. These speakers produce a much clearer sound and work simultaneously to provide higher sound quality and a louder volume overall. This makes the device far more enjoyable for listening to music, audiobooks, or movies.

Wi-Fi Connectivity

Virtually every iPad since the first one came with the ability to connect to Wi-Fi. This is what made the device so attractive. It became known as the ultimate browsing tool and mini-computer that could be used anywhere that had Wi-Fi available. When they launched the iPad Air 2, however, Apple introduced a new feature to the Wi-Fi connectivity. The Wi-Fi can now connect to "AC," which is the fastest connection option available in routers. Not all routers are equipped with this connection, but for those that are, your iPad will pick this connection over any other. The device will naturally and automatically favor the fastest connection, making browsing the Internet and using Wi-Fi-based applications even easier and faster for you.

In addition to having the AC connection available, they introduced "MIMO." MIMO stands for "multiple-in, multiple-out," meaning that your device has multiple antennas on it to connect to Wi-Fi, and it will use as many as possible. The more antennas and sensors that are connected to the router, the faster your Internet speed will be. You can compare this to dial-up or older Internet connections that were based on a single antenna, which was extremely slow. Nowadays, you can connect with as many as all of the antennas in the entire device to maximize your Internet speeds. Every aspect of your iPad's connectivity has been maximized for speed. This is even truer for the iOS 12 update, which now features even faster Internet and performance speeds than before.

Bluetooth 4.0

Bluetooth technology allows for wireless communications between devices; for example, from your iPad to a pair of Bluetooth speakers. You can also use other Bluetooth devices, such as wireless keyboards. Bluetooth "4.0" means that your iPad comes equipped with the latest Bluetooth technology, allowing it to connect to any Bluetooth-capable device and to experience the highest quality connection between the two. It eliminates potential interruptions or interferences between the connection that might temporarily block sound or produce a shoddy connection between your iPad and the other device that you want to connect to.

4G LTE and Assisted GPS

Not all iPads come standard with this feature. However, there are specific models of the iPad that are sold as "cellular" iPads. These models come equipped with the ability to use cell phone companies to receive wireless Internet without being connected to a Wi-Fi router. This means that when you are in cellular range but out of Wi-Fi range, you can rely on your LTE connection to provide you with browsing capabilities.

The cellular models of the device include what is called an Assisted GPS chip. This means that your device is capable of using GPS at any given moment so long as there is cellular connectivity available. It can pinpoint exactly where the iPad is and give you directions to virtually anywhere you desire to go.

Accelerometer, Gyroscope, and Compass

Inside your iPad, there is an accelerometer, gyroscope, and compass. These work together with the Maps application to provide you with the ability to track where you are going, how fast, and what direction you are heading. The accelerometer is able to track your movement, and it uses the support of the gyroscope to refine the tracking process.

This means that it gets a precise insight as to how fast you are moving, allowing your device to know whether you are traveling by foot, bike, or vehicle. It also relies on the compass to determine what direction you are heading. In cellular devices, these three additions support the function of the Assisted GPS, allowing your device to provide you with accurate directions to where you are going.

App Store

Every Apple device comes equipped with the App Store, and the same is true for your iPad. The App Store on the iPad comes stocked with several third-party developer applications that make your device even more functional. In fact, these applications are the reason why most people want the Apple devices. These applications make it even more versatile and user-friendly, giving you a completely customizable experience.

Expansive Flash Storage and iCloud

The iPad comes with flash storage built in, as well as the ability to access iCloud for additional storage options. The cloud storage comes as an equal-opportunity feature for all Apple devices and works interchangeably, allowing you to save things to it on one device and access it later on another device. The flash storage is the built-in storage that is specific to your device. This storage can be shared with other devices by backing it up to iCloud or emailing documents over, but otherwise, it is exclusive to your iPad. The flash storage ranges from 16GB to 128GB, depending on the model you purchase. Each one will come with the opportunity to purchase a device with more or less storage. Those with smaller storage are cheaper, but they also won't be able to store as much data directly on the device. Those with larger storage spaces are more expensive, but they are capable of storing a lot more applications, documents, photographs, and media on the device itself.

10-Hour Battery Life

iPads have the ability to last up to 10 hours on battery power. The actual battery lifespan will depend on what you are doing with the device and how long you are using it, but a 10-hour battery life is usually the standard. Things that affect your battery life include activities such as using LTE or Wi-Fi, streaming movies or music, using a higher brightness, and such. Activities like basic browsing and reading books take up significantly less power and can, therefore, make your device's battery last a lot longer.

Included in the Box

What comes in the box for every iPad, regardless of what generation or model you purchase, is standard. The box will include your iPad, a Lightning-to-USB cable, a wall adapter, and a quick start guide. This is everything you need to begin using your iPad device right away.

Chapter 2
New Features

The new features that are being included in iOS 12 are incredible. Some are similar to what you have already experienced with the iOS 11, whereas others are completely different. In this chapter, we are going to explore all of the unique features that your new iOS 12 is equipped with.

Faster and More Responsive

As a result of the updates to the operating system that you will receive with iOS 12, you will have the opportunity to have an even faster and more responsive experience with your iPad. Considering the fact that iPads are already built to be as quick and functional as possible, these upgraded features mean that your device just got way better.

Your device will now have further-improved Wi-Fi connectivity. Your Internet browsing speeds, downloading speeds, and Internet usage speeds will operate as quickly as the router will allow for, meaning you have the capacity to have an incredibly fast online experience with your iPad. Streaming services, browser loading, and application functions will all perform much faster than before.

Another way that the performance and speed of your device have been improved is in its offline functions. Apps now launch faster, your keyboard will pop up and function quicker, and it is even faster now to swipe to your camera from the lock screen. This means that using your device is even more efficient than ever before. You will never have to worry about missing another beautiful picture again, as you can launch your camera instantaneously and capture images immediately.

Since this is the launch of a completely upgraded operating system, moving from #11 to #12, Apple has placed a large emphasis on performance speed and functionality. They have also ensured that these features are improved on all devices, from as far back as the 2nd generation iPad to the latest models. This means that even if you have an older device, you will still have access to the improved speed and performance features that the new iOS 12 will become available with.

Smoother Animations

Your device comes equipped with many standard animations. Now, as a result of having faster processing and performance speeds, these animations will be smoother than ever before. Scrolling will appear to be seamless, transitioning between applications will be an extremely smooth process, and virtually any other animation will be smoother. For example, if you tap and hold an application to move it into a folder, the animation of moving the application into the folder will be a lot smoother and will feature less lag. This leads to more accurate performance, easier functionality, and—let's be honest—a more enjoyable visual experience.

FaceTime Upgrades

Apple prides itself on its FaceTime application and always seeks to make it better and more useful for Apple users. The FaceTime application has long been used for everything, from conference calling for business teams to calling family and sharing face-to-face experiences with your loved ones.

iOS 12 has been generous in creating an even more enjoyable FaceTime experience for users. For example, you can now host up to 32 people in your conference calls. This means that if you are a business owner or are managing a business team, you no longer have to conduct your conference calls or webinars over expensive third-party applications. Instead, you can simply use your iPad. If you are a part of a family that is spread out across the world, you can use this FaceTime feature to connect all of you together and share a valuable face-to-face time that may otherwise be a challenge to arrange.

In addition to larger calling capabilities, FaceTime has been made more efficient and effective for seamless calling experiences. Now, the user speaking can be amplified in "Focus View," where their screen becomes front and center in the conference call. Additionally, you can now add people mid-call with ringless notifications. This means that those people in the call no longer have to listen to the interference of the ringing sound as they wait for the added caller to answer the call. Instead, the call can continue with no noise or interference from the added caller. Also, you can launch these calls from group messenger chats, automatically including everyone in the chat into the call. This means you no longer have to independently invite every individual into the group call. Instead, it can be launched with a single action.

FaceTime has also become more enjoyable with new features that allow you to customize the viewing experience. You can now use Animoji, the new Memoji, and even camera filters in your calls. This can make casual and friendly chats even more enjoyable, adding a new layer of fun and experience to the call. In addition to these functions, you can also use text effects and built-in shapes on your video. There are even third-party sticker applications that can now be downloaded and used on your camera. Although these features are not exactly a necessity, they certainly make the experience of using your device far more enjoyable.

Lastly, Apple is always very adamant about keeping things as secure as possible. They value a private experience and your private information, and they seek to keep your experience as safe as possible. That being said, FaceTime now includes private end-to-end encryption. This means that your conversations remain completely private and are impossible to be viewed by anyone other than those who are actively participating in the call. That way, you may be sure that your calling experience is completely private and that no one is hacking into your call or accidentally dialing in to potentially receive sensitive information.

Messages Upgrades

Apple is all about connecting people. Naturally, they have added many upgrades to the iMessage application. The Apple-exclusive messenger application now includes many more incredible features, making it even more interactive and entertaining for sharing conversations with loved ones. The most notable change made to the iMessages application is to the in-app camera and the way it works. It now has many more features that make taking and sharing photographs far more enjoyable and interactive.

Following the trends of modern social media updates, the camera in your iMessages app now features filters, text effects, shapes, and even the ability to add stickers and Animoji's directly to the photographs and videos. This makes sharing photo and video with your loved ones a more interactive and fun experience. You can now capture and customize images and share exactly what you are doing at any given time through the power of image or video.

As the filters are now built-in, you can apply them and use them directly in the application itself while you are taking photographs. Then, after you take the picture or image, you can also lay text effects, speech bubbles, stickers from third-party application downloads (see below), and Animoji or Memoji graphics over the image or video. This allows you to customize the photograph and have even more fun with the experience.

Animoji and Memoji Upgrades

When Apple launched the iPhone 8 Plus and iPhone X, they launched a feature called Animoji. These are animated emojis that you can make yourself through your camera and a variety of unique features on your device. Now, with the launch of iOS 12, they are releasing what is called Memoji. This is a similar application, except that it scans your face and creates a custom emoji that looks just like you. Plus, if you don't feel it is accurate enough, you can adjust its features and make it even more realistic.

In addition to introducing Memoji, which is accessible through your emoji keyboard on any application, you can also now enjoy a few extra upgrades to Animoji. iOS 12 will include the release of the filters of a T-rex, a koala, a tiger, and a ghost. You will also be able to create animations that last up to 30 seconds long. These Animoji's and Memoji's can be sent independently, or they can be uploaded to a photo or video as a customization feature. You can also use them in the FaceTime application to customize your live feed video stream in any one-to-one or conference call.

iMessage Sticker Packs

Being able to add stickers to your photographs or videos in the native iMessage app has never been a feature before iOS 12. Now, Apple has introduced the opportunity to download third-party sticker packages. These packs are designed by third-party developers and are downloadable in the App Store. Upon downloading them, you can load them into your iMessages application and lay them over any photograph or video taken with your in-app camera.

You can also use these sticker features in FaceTime, once again giving you the option to further customize your experience. These stickers can also be "clicked" into place on video feeds, allowing it to stay locked into a certain part, causing the sticker to move around on camera.

Screen Time Upgrades

For many years, the amount of screen time we experience has been debated, studied, and explored. It is no secret that screen addiction is a real issue that the modern world faces and that the tech industry that is responsible for designing the screens often gets the rough end of the stick. Apple has always been passionate about encouraging users to minimize screen time, which is why so many of their updates work to offer more hands-free solutions.

In addition to hands-free solutions, which you will learn more about in "Siri Suggestions and Updates," they have also included a Screen Time application. This application is available on your device and gives you plenty of detailed information about how much time you are spending on your device, including how many hours you've spent each day and week using specific applications and how many times you check your device per hour.

As well as being able to track and monitor your screen time, the Screen Time application allows you to actually manage your experience. Through the application, you can now automatically limit screen time in general, limit the amount of time spent in certain applications, and otherwise customize your experience to encourage yourself to put your device down more often.

If you are a parent, Screen Time also features parental controls that have the capacity to prevent children from using certain applications, as well as using the device during certain hours (called "downtime" on your device). It also includes an "always allow" access to certain applications. If your child reaches their time limit on a certain application, they have to request access on the device and be given the access by a parent to receive any more time. This means that you have far more control over your child's device usage than ever before.

Your iPad will recognize each individual user through their Apple ID information, which will allow it to further customize the experience from user to user. This means that even if you are sharing a device with family members, you each can still have your own custom settings in place to manage and monitor screen time.

Notification Upgrades

Although it seems minimal, notifications are a large part of our experiences with a device. If you think about it, you will likely receive tens and hundreds of notifications on a daily basis. Studies have shown that these constant notifications can create a type of anxiety in users, resulting in them feeling like they are constantly "on call." This anxiety can actually lead to heightened amounts of stress, which is extremely unhealthy if it is experienced for a prolonged period of time.

Apple has introduced new notification features in iOS 12 that allow you to customize your notification settings, giving you the opportunity to have more down time in which you are not being bothered or impacted by a device that's consistently giving you notifications.

One of the changed features in the notifications is your ability to group them. Now, rather than having long notification threads from a single text conversation or application, you can have them grouped together so that you can see them all at once. This makes it much easier to locate the exact notification you want to receive and helps to prevent you from missing any that may get lost in the sea of notifications that Apple devices currently experience.

Additionally, you can actually set notifications to be considered "Critical Alert." This means that your notification will push a notification to you no matter what, even if you have your device set to Do Not Disturb. These alerts are great for anyone who wants to receive alerts from important notifications, such as messages from a health care provider, or a reminder to measure certain health levels, such as blood pressure or blood sugar.

Alongside "Critical Alert," you can also silence the notifications from specific devices. This means that you'll be able to tell certain applications not to push notifications with alerts. While they will still show you the notification, they will not ring or vibrate on your phone. This is great for less important alerts, such as social media updates and the like.

Being able to customize your notifications means that it is now significantly easier for you to use your device. You no longer have to worry about missing important notifications, you have greater control over which notifications you receive and don't, and you can have greater customization options over your user experience.

Do Not Disturb Options

The ability to have a customizable Do Not Disturb feature is far more exciting and beneficial than one might think. Do Not Disturb is the mode that allows you to prevent your device from receiving any notification alerts or anything similar. The device is completely silenced. You can do even more now with Do Not Disturb, and the first major advantage is that it has become far more effective.

In previous versions of the iOS, your screen would still light up and display a short blurb about the notification that you received. Now, when your device is in Do Not Disturb, you will not experience the screen lighting up, nor would small notification highlights appear on your lock screen. Instead, they will be hidden in the open home screen and will only be shown to you if you intentionally go to look for them. This is great for people who tend to check their phones when they wake up in the middle of the night and then become distracted by the notifications they receive, thinking that it's extremely important to answer right away.

Another cool feature in the iOS 12 is that you can have Do Not Disturb mode on overnight and set it to automatically turn off in the morning when you unlock your phone. This way, you do not accidentally leave your device in Do Not Disturb mode and miss important updates and notifications throughout the day.

Lastly, Do Not Disturb mode now comes complete with a feature that allows you to schedule your Do Not Disturb mode. This means you can turn it on and have it automatically turn off at a specific time. This is great if you want to take a nap, go into a meeting or an appointment, or otherwise unplug for a few hours. You will not receive any notifications or alerts until the time is up and Do Not Disturb mode automatically turns back off.

Augmented Reality

Apple is passionate about augmented reality and has been searching for ways to incorporate it even more. They have included massive upgrades to their augmented reality experience, now including the opportunity to use it for tools such as measuring things, leaving art around the world, and even to access certain unique features in standard applications on your device such as Files or Safari.

The Measure App will be explained later in Chapter 4, but this application allows you to use the augmented reality feature to measure real-life objects. This turns your phone into a handy little device!

You can also use what is called persistent multi-user experiences. This means that you can create a piece of art, take a picture, or film a short video and lock it into place in a physical area. Then, any time a fellow Apple user comes to that place and uses their augmented reality application, they will be able to view the artwork that you have left. There are also applications that utilize this feature to create games that can be viewed in reality through the camera lens and played by multiple people.

The new ARKit2 software that is included in the iOS 12 operating system upgrade is also created to feature better face tracking, scene reflection, and 3D object recognition. This means your device can now begin to tell objects apart, recognizing each individual piece of the landscape. Previously, it only saw in 2D.

In everyday applications such as Mail, Files, Messages, and Safari, augmented reality can now be used as well. Each native application will come with unique features that allow you to incorporate augmented reality into the experience. The opportunities with augmented reality on iOS 12 exceed that with any previous iOS device, and it is truly beginning to show the capability of augmented reality in our lives!

Photo Upgrades

The Photos application is already a user-friendly application. Now, in iOS 12, your Photos application is even better than ever. A new "For You" tab allows you to see your memories, shared album activity, and best moments all in your own library. The application will also provide recommendations on what effects to use so that you can enhance your photos for an even better viewing experience.

Another incredible feature is that your device will be able to identify when something meaningful is happening. If you and your family take a trip or attend an event, for example, your device will recognize this experience, as well as the faces of the people in your photographs. Then, it will provide a suggestion of whether to share these images with the people it has detected. If you have set up Face Recognition for these people, it will even offer their direct contact information so that you can send it directly and instantaneously without having to do much on your own.

Expanding on the Face Recognition feature, your device will also begin recognizing anytime someone sends you images through an iMessage. Then, if it recognizes that you have similar photographs from the same trip or event in your device, you will be shown these as a suggestion to share back. This makes sharing experiences with loved ones far easier, as you no longer have to scroll extensively to find the pictures you want to share. Your device will perform the search for you.

Finally, Apple has introduced a new feature to the Photos app that allows you to search for specific photos with greater ease. With iOS 12, you can now search for keywords, and your iPad will produce any images that match them. And, to make it even better, they also introduced multiple keyword searches. This means that you can input several keywords into the search bar and discover the exact photos you are looking for. For example, if you type "vacation" and "skiing," your device will automatically locate and show you all of the photographs where you are skiing on vacation.

Portrait Upgrades

In addition to upgrading the app in which you view your photos, the iOS 12 also comes with upgrades to your camera. The part of your camera being specifically impacted by this is your portrait mode. All of the devices that have the capacity to take portrait mode photographs will now take clearer images that are of significantly higher quality.

In portrait mode, your camera will now generate what is called a "mask" any time it detects the highlighted person or object that you wish to separate from the rest of the scene. This makes it easier for your phone to do the separation, meaning you will have a more even and clean blur line around your subject. You may have noticed that until now, many portrait mode photographs had inaccurate lines around the subject you were photographing, often resulting in pieces of the background being as clear as the subject and taking away from the quality of the photo. This will not happen anymore with the new mask feature.

As well as having clearer photographs with cleaner lines, you will also have better lighting in your portrait mode photographs. Now, you will have a clearer and more vibrant lighting on your subject, as well as a slightly darker cast over the background. This equals an even greater separating effect, resulting in a clearer and more enjoyable photograph.

Siri Suggestions and Upgrades

Ever since it was introduced, Siri has been a major part of Apple devices. This built-in assistant has continued to get better with every new operating system upgrade or launch, resulting in it being able to do more and support more. Of course, Siri is also receiving some new capabilities with the new iOS 12!

One of the biggest features they have upgraded with Siri in the iOS 12 is Siri's ability to provide you with suggestions. Previously, Siri would only provide you with suggestions when you asked for them. Now, you will receive a notification that allows you to see what Siri suggests at any given time. These suggestions will also be much quicker. When you actually ask for a suggestion, Siri will also respond quicker and have several more suggestions than older versions of Siri did.

Additionally, Siri can now recognize and learn your routines. This means that it can provide you with recommended shortcuts that make living your life easier. (You will learn more about shortcuts in Chapter 4 under the "Shortcut App" subsection.) Using these recommended shortcuts can result in your device performing many functions for you, from turning on devices in your smart home to texting people a specific message for you.

Siri is also now capable of providing you with even more updates than ever before. You can now ask Siri to inform you about updates on current motorsport stats, relevant and recent celebrity facts, information about food, and more. It also features several more languages in its dictionary, meaning Siri can now support 40 language pairings to help bilingual individuals translate directly through their device using spoken word. Additionally, Siri can now help you search for passwords and photographs through voice commands. It is truly becoming one of the most powerful assets of Apple devices.

Enhanced Privacy and Security

Apple is extremely focused on creating safe and private user experiences for individuals. They seek to protect your privacy and always ensure that your experience is not putting you at risk for hackers, fraud, or other such dangers.

With the new iOS 12 upgrades, you will now have even better privacy and security on your iPad. One of the features that Apple has included is called "enhanced tracking prevention." This means that websites you visit can no longer track information about you or your system to target ads directly towards you across your entire mobile browsing experience. Safari itself will be the best browser to use with your Apple device to gain full access to this protected browsing experience, as they have upgraded the app to have better security all around.

You may have noticed that your iPad gives you suggested passwords anytime you are creating a new password. These randomly automated passwords are designed to create strong and difficult to replicate password keys that prevent hackers from getting into your accounts. Apple has made it so that these automated passwords now feature even more security, meaning there is even less of a chance of being hacked by others.

Additionally, you will now have access to autofill suggestions that are capable of remembering one-time passcodes you may be sent. This means you no longer have to remember the code in one application and input it into another. Instead, you will be able to rely on your device to autofill the code for you.

Finally, you will be able to easily share your passwords from your iPad to other Apple iOS devices, meaning you don't have to worry about remembering your passwords anymore. If you use the automated passwords that are typically a lot harder to remember, you don't have to fear that you will forget the password and would no longer be able to access your account without changing the password all over again. Your devices will do it all for you. You will even be able to recall third-party passwords, which can now be stored in the QuickType bar in Safari.

Updates to Built-In Applications

Three of the applications that come built-in to your device are now going to be improved even further. They include Apple Books, Stocks, and Voice Memos.

Apple Books (formerly known as iBooks) has had a complete redesign that made it much easier for you to discover new books, as well as locate and listen to or read your current books. The books can now be stored in a "Reading Now" tab that populates itself any time you begin reading a new book. That way, you can effortlessly access your latest read, as opposed to having to search for it. It also makes it far easier to organize your collection.

Stocks has been redesigned as well, giving you more information about the stock market. You can now easily view all prices briefly in your customized watch list. Then, simply tap the chosen price, and you can get an interactive detailed chart to view the information on. This is the first time that Apple has created an update that will make Stocks available to iPad users.

The Voice Memo redesign means voice memos are now fully accessible on iPad. Previously, the application was limited for iPad users, meaning you couldn't get the full range of the application. You can now use Voice Memo to capture reminders, edit class lectures, or even share family moments. You can also record and save them to iCloud, then later access them on your MacBook to be able to customize the recording even better.

iPad Gestures

On iOS 12 for the iPad, there are more gestures available, making it even easier for you to navigate your device. Now, you can quickly swipe up from the bottom of the screen to return to the home screen, swipe down from the top-right corner to the bottom-left corner to access the Control Center, and more.

New Dictionaries

Always seeking to make their device more user-friendly for everyone, Apple has added three additional languages to the iOS dictionary. These new bilingual dictionaries include Arabic and English bilingual, Hindi and English bilingual, and Hebrew and English bilingual.

Thesaurus

In addition to upgrading their dictionaries to include even more languages, Apple has also included a new Thesaurus for their devices. Currently, the Thesaurus only supports the English language. However, you can now use it to help you when you are writing things out as it will support you in receiving synonyms and related words on your device. If you use your device for educational purposes, or if you are simply looking to expand your vocabulary, this will be a powerful addition to have on your device.

Chapter 3
Getting Started with iOS 12 and Customizing Features

There are clearly a lot of updates coming with the new iOS! Everything has been given a redesign or upgrades, ensuring that your experience would be even more enjoyable. Apple has sought to make their devices more user-friendly, easier to integrate with one another, more secure and protected, and far more interactive and enjoyable. Of course, any time we experience new upgrades to a device, there is always a bit of a learning curve that we need to endure.

In this chapter, we are going to take a deeper look at how you can take advantage of all of these new features and upgrades. While some, such as the Siri upgrades, are simply ones that you can explore on your own with voice commands, others require a little more to get started. Below, you are going to find more about everything you need to know to get acquainted with your iOS 12 operating system upgrade. This will help you get maximum use from your device and enjoy all of the new features being added to it.

How to Upgrade to iOS 12

At this book's time of writing, iOS 12 has not yet been released to the general public. There has been a lot of commentary about it from Apple in keynote speeches, as well as information circulating about the operating system. However, we are still waiting for it to make its official debut. As of this moment, iOS 12 is in its beta stages. It is speculated that it will be launched to the public in September of 2018, alongside the new iPhone and iPad devices that will become available for Apple's annual product launch.

Once it does become available, however, it is extremely easy to upgrade to iOS 12. Simply log in to your device and, following the launch of the new operating system, a prompt should come up, encouraging you to download the new operating system. This can take a few days after the launch, so give it some time.

If you want to see if it is available yet despite not having received any notification, you can check through accessing your settings. To do this, enter your settings menu and go to the "General" option. Then, choose "Software Update." If the iOS 12 update is available to you, it will become visible here. Simply select "Update," and it will begin to update for you immediately.

iOS 12 Beta

Currently, iOS 12 is available as a beta application. This means that, if you apply, you can download the beta software to your device and begin exploring and using the new features of the iOS 12. This is an awesome opportunity to get a live and in-person experience with the new operating system. However, it does have its drawbacks, too.

One of the pros of having the beta on your device is that you get to experience all of the new features right away. Additionally, being a part of the beta launch means that you can provide real-time feedback to Apple through the beta application, which helps them ensure that the beta is fully proofed and ready for launch when the new operating system officially goes public. This can be a pretty cool experience to be involved in. Plus, you get the bragging rights of saying that you have already had the operating system in place long before it officially came out, which is a fun aspect as well.

A con to having the beta downloaded on your device, however, is that you are putting your device at risk of any bugs or defects that the operating system may currently carry in its beta stages. Because it is not officially proofed and ready for launch, the developers are still working on making sure that it works properly. While it is not extremely common, some people who have downloaded beta programs in the past have experienced their device breaking down and irreparable as a result. If you are not careful, you can lose everything, and your device can become virtually useless. It is important that you take some time to consider whether this risk is worth it for you or not.

If you do decide that you want to go through with being one of the beta testers, it is imperative that you back up your entire device before you download and launch the new operating system. Additionally, it is typically recommended that you run it on an old or secondary device, instead of putting it directly on your new and most frequently used device. That way, if you do end up having your device bugged and it breaks, the possible damage would not be as great.

To download the operating system early and become an official beta tester of iOS 12, you will want to go to beta.apple.com. There, you will be guided through the process of applying for, installing, and using the new operating system in its beta stages.

Navigating Your New Features

The primary emphasis in the new iOS 12 features is on Memoji, Screen Time, Group FaceTime, Notifications, Augmented Reality, Siri, and Do Not Disturb mode. In this section, we are going to discover what these are and how you can use and set up these new features.

Memoji

Animoji is a feature where you can create an animated emoji on your iPhone X. You will now be able to use these on iPad as well, via your iMessage application. To access the new features, you will want to tap into the Animoji section in your iMessages application and begin by taking an image or a short 30-second video clip of your face. Then, you will be given the opportunity to completely customize the feature. You will find far more interactive experiences here to create an Animoji that perfectly resembles your personality or mood at the moment. You can even have it copy what your tongue is doing or capture you while you are winking—these are two new features, as the sensors had not been sensitive enough to capture these particular motions in the original Animoji application.

They have also added a new feature called Memoji. This allows you to create emojis that look exactly like you. You can customize hairstyle, skin tone, and more. It starts by taking a picture or a short 30-second video clip of your face, then it uses built-in sensors to design an animated emoji that looks just like you! You can even add a cartoon version of the Memoji (or Animoji) to the videos that you send through messenger.

Exploring the new Animoji and Memoji features will be best done if you simply play with the application. There are so many options and features to choose from that we may be able to write an entire book on just Animoji, and Memoji features one of these days!

Screen Time

Everyone is talking about screen addiction these days, and Apple has set out to do something about it with their Screen Time feature. The new setting labeled "Screen Time" can be located in your Control Center panel, which can now be accessed by swiping down from the right-top corner section of the screen.

The Screen Time application will provide you with a full report on how your screen time has been over the past 24 hours, as well as over the past week. It will tell you how much more or less that time is compared to previous days and weeks, helping you track how much time you are spending "plugged in" to your iPad. This application will tell you information such as your total screen time, how long you've used each particular app and the number of times you have picked up your phone in a one-hour span.

Through the Screen Time application, you can also access a setting called "Manage Screen Time" displayed at the bottom of the application. Here, you can set unique permissions for each application which will cause them to shut down and lock you out after a certain number of minutes or hours spent on the application, all within a 24-hour span, or consecutively. You can also control this from user to user, meaning you can ensure that your children are not using the device longer than allowed. The parental control section will also show you how much screen time your children have had on the Apple device and which applications they are spending their time in the most.

Apple has always been a company that encourages people to set down their devices and spend more time enjoying their life. For that reason, it makes sense that they would begin adding features to help people become more mindful about their screen usage time and how they can reduce it.

Do Not Disturb

Although it is small and insignificant, the new Do Not Disturb mode settings are actually incredible upgrades for Apple devices. You can actually go into your settings for Do Not Disturb mode, accessible through the Control Center, and set a timer for how long you want the mode activated.

Additionally, when it is activated, Do Not Disturb will not even provide silent notifications for anything aside from "Critical Alert" notifications (which can be set in the Control Panel also, see below). This means that your screen will not light up and your lock screen will not display the notifications like it did previously. Thus, if you are the kind of person who wakes up in the middle of the night and uses their phone to check the time, you won't be tempted by the notifications to begin browsing your device. Instead, it will seem as though you have no notifications.

Notifications

The new notification features enable you to group notifications and set Critical Alerts so that your phone will inform you of the notification even if it is set to Do Not Disturb. To do this, you can simply tap and hold any notification that comes in and choose to set it to a specific group, or else change the level of urgency for the notification.

Siri will also recognize your notifications and begin offering you suggested groups and alert settings based on the information it gathers. You can even use Siri to set these by simply saying "Hey Siri, group (x) notifications." If you are unsure as to how, or if Siri does not seem to be understanding you, you can always ask it to help you use the command. Simply say, "Hey Siri, can you help me group my notifications?"

Live Listen

A cool feature that is built-in to the new iOS 12 is called Live Listen. If the place you are in is too loud, this new feature makes it possible for you to listen to someone across the table from you, or in the room with you, better.

Simply connect your AirPod headphones to the device and set it on the table, then set the device to "Live Listen" which can be accessed in the Control Panel menu. Now, any time that person speaks, you can hear them, and the noise in the room won't be a problem anymore.

Setting up the new features on your iPad with iOS 12 takes some getting used to. However, once you play with it for some time, you will find that it becomes significantly easier for you to use. If you find that it is particularly challenging for you to remember all of the new features, you can always practice just using one at a time and starting there! This might make it easier for you to really get the hang of your new operating system and gain full functionality of it. And, of course, you can always use this eBook to help you along the way!

Chapter 4
New iOS 12 Apps and Customization

With the launch of iOS 12 comes not only updated applications but also entirely new applications as well. Along with the new software and features that they have installed in this new operating system, Apple has launched two new noteworthy applications, as well as two significantly upgraded applications. Let's take a look at what they are and how they can be used!

Measure App

The Measure app was able to be introduced after Apple included an improved augmented reality software into their operating system. This software is called "ARKit2." This means that the augmented reality is accounted for even when you are not using an official augmented reality application. You will get to experience one of the coolest features of this upgrade in the new Measure app, which lets you measure things with your device through the augmented reality software.

This application will come as a stock on your device with the upgrade. To use it, simply launch the application and give it permission to use your camera. You will be able to point it at whatever you desire to measure. By drawing a straight line in the air, it will measure the space for you, allowing you to know exactly how tall, long, or deep things are. For example, you can measure a new couch before bringing it home to make sure that it will actually fit in your space. Or, you can measure the height of your child as they grow up.

This new tool is both a fun example of what augmented reality can mean for us, as well as a really handy feature to have in your pocket at any given time. While you may not use it too often, it will certainly be useful when the need arises!

Shortcuts App

The Shortcuts app allows you to perform many incredible tasks with the support of Siri. This application allows you to program Siri with an action sequence that is based on a specific command. Thus, when you tell Siri to complete the action, it will go ahead and do it all for you.

A great example of this would be to set up a Shortcut action called "Go Home." This feature, when used, could automatically text your significant other to let them know that you are on your way home. It would then launch the Maps application and give you your route home, all while also telling your significant other the time left until your expected arrival time.

There are many fascinating Shortcuts you can create in the Shortcut application that will make using your phone hands-free with the assistance of Siri. You can even program it to set the temperature in your home, give you directions, set a specific playlist, control certain smart home devices, and more. The opportunities with the Shortcut application are endless.

To create your own Shortcuts, simply launch the application and tap "Create New Shortcut." The application will then guide you through the process of choosing what action sequence you want to occur, and from there, to creating a launch command for the action sequence.

Siri and Applications

Siri, with applications in general, is going to be significantly different with the iOS 12. As a result of the new Shortcuts app, you will now be able to do so much more with Siri. You can use it to group notifications, customize settings on your device, and experience your device more hands-free and much easier than ever before. It will also now track your routines with your device, then recommend Shortcuts that you can set to make the user experience even more seamless.

Apple is working toward making Siri your ultimate hands-free assistant so that you can get the most out of your device while doing less. It appears that the developers are working toward making your device capable of doing so much more so that you no longer have to perform as many functions or complete as many tasks to maximize your device's capabilities. Instead, you will be able to simply ask Siri to do it for you. The great thing about this, too, is that Siri can synchronize across all of your devices and communicate between the two.

Apple Books

One application that has been completely redesigned and reintroduced in iOS 12 is the Apple Books application. Formerly known as iBooks, Apple Books will now feature all of your downloaded reading and listening material and display it in an entirely new way. The new "Reading Now" tab available at the top of the application allows you to navigate to the book you have been listening to or reading most recently, making it easier for you to locate what you have already been reading.

You will also notice that Apple Books is much more efficient at recommending titles and allowing you to browse for new reads. The genres have been organized in a more structured manner, and the books have been designed to make it extremely simple for your iPad to locate and recommend new reading materials based off of what you have already read in the past. This makes using the application much more enjoyable and customized than ever before.

Conclusion

Congratulations on purchasing and reading this book!

The book, *iOS 12 for iPad: The Answer to All Your IOS Questions,* is designed to help you, as an iPad user, get the most out of your device with Apple's latest upgrades and integrations. With this iOS 12 operating system guide, you can now have full access to all of the knowledge you need about the new features on your device.

I hope that this guide has helped explain what to expect with your upgraded system, how it will impact and benefit you as an iPad user, and how you can take full advantage of all of the new features on your device. From showing you the basic features and how each one will be upgraded in the new iOS 12 to showing you how to use these features and what you can do to customize them, I have tried to populate this book with as much information as possible.

The next step is to await the launch of iOS 12! After that, you can begin using the new operating system on your device. Remember to keep this guide handy so that any time you are curious about what a certain feature is or how to get the most out of it, you'll have immediate access to this information!

Lastly, if you enjoyed this book, please take the time to leave a review. Your honest feedback would be appreciated.

Thank you and be sure to enjoy the brand-new iOS 12 experience!

www.ingramcontent.com/pod-product-compliance
Lightning Source LLC
Chambersburg PA
CBHW070858070326
40690CB00009B/1901